The Wisdom of
NARNIA

C. S. LEWIS

ILLUSTRATIONS BY PAULINE BAYNES

HarperCollins*Publishers*

NARNIA®

Abbreviations used in this book:

MN—*The Magician's Nephew*
LWW—*The Lion, the Witch and the Wardrobe*
HHB—*The Horse and His Boy*
PC—*Prince Caspian*
VDT—*The Voyage of the Dawn Treader*
SC—*The Silver Chair*
LB—*The Last Battle*

Page references used herein are based on the digest paperback editions of these books published by HarperCollins in 1994.

The seven Chronicles of Narnia (in reading order) were first published in Great Britain as follows:
The Magician's Nephew copyright © 1955 by C.S. Lewis Pte. Ltd.
The Lion, the Witch and the Wardrobe copyright © 1950 by C.S. Lewis Pte. Ltd.
The Horse and His Boy copyright © 1954 by C.S. Lewis Pte. Ltd.
Prince Caspian copyright © 1951 by C.S. Lewis Pte. Ltd.
The Voyage of the Dawn Treader copyright © 1952 by C.S. Lewis Pte. Ltd.
The Silver Chair copyright © 1953 by C.S. Lewis Pte. Ltd.
The Last Battle copyright © 1956 by C.S. Lewis Pte. Ltd.

The Wisdom of Narnia
Copyright © 2001 by C.S. Lewis Pte. Ltd.
Illustrations by Pauline Baynes; copyright © 1950, 1951, 1952, 1953, 1954, 1955, 1956 by C.S. Lewis Pte. Ltd.

For information address HarperCollins Children's Books, a division of HarperCollins Publishers, 1350 Avenue of the Americas, New York, NY 10019.
Printed with permission from HarperCollins Publishers.
www.narnia.com
ISBN 10: 0-310-60173-8
ISBN 13: 978-0-310-60173-9

❖

2 3 4 5 6 7 8 9 10

The Wisdom of Narnia

Captivated by the spirited adventures of C. S. Lewis's *The Chronicles of Narnia*, generations of readers have also been touched and inspired by their timeless wisdom, simple truths, and gentle humor. We come to understand, through excerpts from all seven books, the power of this special place that has been so important to readers for over fifty years.

There's nothing to beat good freshwater fish if you eat it when it has been alive half an hour ago and has come out of the pan half a minute ago.

LWW: 74

PC: 83

Simple Pleasures

To sleep under the stars, to drink nothing but well water and to live chiefly on nuts and wild fruit, was a strange experience for Caspian after his bed with silken sheets in a tapestried chamber at the castle, with meals laid out on gold and silver dishes in the anteroom, and attendants ready at his call. But he had never enjoyed himself more. Never had sleep been more refreshing nor food tasted more savory.

PC: 84

PC: 131

LB: 43

When it was almost dark Tirian heard a light pitter-patter of feet and saw some small creatures coming toward him. . . . Then, in a moment, they were all standing up on their hind legs, laying their cool paws on his knees and giving his knees snuffly animal kisses. . . . They fed him with oat-cakes and fresh butter, and then with some more wine.

"Now hand up the water," said the first Mouse, "and I'll wash the King's face. There is blood on it."

LB: 42–44

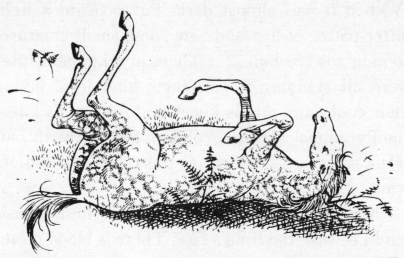

HHB: 210

"We're free Narnians, Hwin and I, and I suppose, if you're running away to Narnia, you want to be one too. In that case Hwin isn't *your* horse any longer. One might just as well say you're *her* human."

—*Bree the Horse*

HHB: 32

MN: 115

All this time the Lion's song, and his stately prowl, to and fro, backward and forward, was going on. . . . When a line of dark firs sprang up on a ridge . . . [Polly] felt that they were connected with a series of deep, prolonged notes which the Lion had sung a second before. And when he burst into a rapid series of lighter notes she was not surprised to see primroses suddenly appearing in every direction. Thus . . . she felt quite certain that all the things were coming (as she said) "out of the Lion's head."

MN: 115

"Send Glenstorm, Sire. No one ever laughed at a Centaur."

—*Trufflehunter*

PC: 178

PC: 185

"As we birds say, nests before eggs."

HHB: 73–74

"See the bear in his own den before you judge of his conditions."

HHB: 65

"Easily in but not easily out, as the lobster said in the lobster pot!"

—*Sallowpad the Raven*

HHB: 63

Uncle Andrew shrugged his shoulders . . . and said:

". . . Leave the little girl to be eaten by wild animals or drowned or starved in the Otherworld or lost there for good. . . . Perhaps before tea time you'd better drop in on Mrs. Plummer and explain that she'll never see her daughter again; because you were afraid to put on a ring."

MN: 29–30

MN: 26

. . . [Digory] took a deep breath, and picked up the ring. And he thought then, as he always thought afterward too, that he could not decently have done anything else.

MN: 30

MN: 5

MN: 125

"Creatures, I give you yourselves," said the strong, happy voice of Aslan. "I give to you forever this land of Narnia. I give you the woods, the fruits, the rivers. I give you the stars and I give you myself. The Dumb Beasts whom I have not chosen are yours also. Treat them gently and cherish them but do not go back to their ways lest you cease to be Talking Beasts. For out of them you were taken and into them you can return. Do not so."

MN: 128

"But what do you want with a tail?" asked Aslan.

"Sir," said the Mouse, "I can eat and sleep and die for my King without one. But a tail is the honor and glory of a Mouse."

PC: 208

PC: 207

"Why have your followers all drawn *their* swords, may I ask?" said Aslan. . . .

"We will not bear the shame of wearing an honor which is denied to the High Mouse."

"Ah!" roared Aslan. "You have conquered me. You have great hearts. Not for the sake of your dignity, Reepicheep, but for the love that is between you and your people . . . you shall have your tail again."

PC: 209

"Welcome, child," he said.

"Aslan," said Lucy, "you're bigger."

"That is because you are older, little one," answered he.

"Not because you are?"

"I am not. But every year you grow, you will find me bigger."

"You need not always be grave. For jokes as well as justice come in with speech."

MN: 129

"Oh dear," said Lucy. "Have I spoiled everything? Do you mean we would have gone on being friends if it hadn't been for this . . . and now we never shall?"

"Child," said Aslan, "did I not explain to you once before that no one is ever told what *would have happened*?"

VDT: 159–160

Peter held the door closed but did not shut it; for, of course, he remembered, as every sensible person does, that you should never never shut yourself up in a wardrobe.

LWW: 53

LWW: 7

If you've been up all night and cried till you have no more tears left in you—you will know that there comes in the end a sort of quietness. You feel as if nothing was ever going to happen again.

When things go wrong, you'll find they usually go on getting worse for some time; but when things once start going right they often go on getting better and better.

MN: 199

What you see and hear depends a good deal on where you are standing: it also depends on what sort of person you are.

MN: 136

SC: 51

Jill held her tongue. (If you don't want other people to know how frightened you are, this is always a wise thing to do; it's your voice that gives you away.)

SC: 212

"I tell you, it *is* an animal," said the Bulldog. "Smell it for yourself."

"Smelling isn't everything," said the Elephant.

"Why," said the Bulldog, "if a fellow can't trust his nose, what is he to trust?"

"Well, his brains, perhaps," she replied mildly.

MN: 143

MN: 141

"Logic!" said the Professor half to himself. "Why don't they teach logic at these schools? There are only three possibilities. Either your sister is telling lies, or she is mad, or she is telling the truth. You know she doesn't tell lies and it is obvious that she is not mad. For the moment then and unless any further evidence turns up, we must assume that she is telling the truth."

LWW: 48

PC: 185

"Whatever we do, don't let's have any *running*. Especially not before supper; and not too soon after it neither."

—*Bulgy Bears*

PC: 90

"Visible we are," said . . . the Chief Monopod. "And what I say is, when chaps are visible, why, they can see one another."

VDT: 168

VDT: 168

"Any pool will do . . ." [said Digory]. "Let's try that one."

"Stop!" said Polly. "Aren't we going to mark *this* pool?"

They . . . turned quite white as they realized the dreadful thing that Digory had just been going to do. For there were any number of pools in the wood, and the pools were all alike and the trees were all alike, so that if they had once left behind the pool that led to our own world without making some sort of landmark, the chances would have been a hundred to one against their ever finding it again.

"If anyone present wishes to make me the subject of his wit, I am very much at his service—with my sword—whenever he has leisure."

—*Reepicheep*

PC: 187

PC: 187

"This is a very great adventure, and no danger seems to me so great as that of knowing . . . I left a mystery behind me through fear."

VDT: 197

"If you are a foe we do not fear you, and if you are a friend your enemies shall be taught the fear of us."

—*Reepicheep*

VDT: 182

VDT: 103

VDT: 93

A Lesson Learned

He had turned into a dragon while he was asleep. Sleeping on a dragon's hoard with greedy, dragonish thoughts in his heart, he had become a dragon himself. . . . An appalling loneliness came over him. He began to see that the others had not really been fiends at all. He began to wonder if he himself had been such a nice person as he had always supposed. . . . The poor dragon that had been Eustace lifted up its voice and wept.

VDT: 91–92

HHB: 177

True Leadership

"For this is what it means to be a king: to be first in every desperate attack and last in every desperate retreat, and when there's hunger in the land . . . to wear finer clothes and laugh louder over a scantier meal than any man in your land."

"The king's under the law, for it's the law makes him a king."
—*King Lune of Archenland*

MN: 76

[Uncle Andrew] seemed a little shrimp of a creature beside the Witch. . . . One good thing about seeing the two together was that you would never again be afraid of Uncle Andrew, any more than you'd be afraid of a worm after you had met a rattlesnake or afraid of a cow after you had met a mad bull.

MN: 75

VDT: 178

It had taken everyone just that half-minute to remember certain dreams they had had—dreams that make you afraid of going to sleep again—and to realize what it would mean to land on a country where dreams come true. . . .

"Row, row," bellowed Caspian. . . . "There are some things no man can face."

VDT: 184

"He called for Tash: Tash has come. . . . People shouldn't call for demons unless they really mean what they say."

—*Poggin the Dwarf*

LB: 94

LB: 151

"[The Witch] has won her heart's desire; she has unwearying strength and endless days like a goddess. But length of days with an evil heart is only length of misery and already she begins to know it. All get what they want; they do not always like it."

—*Aslan*

MN: 190

MN: 59

Instantly a glorious feast appeared on the Dwarfs' knees. . . . But it wasn't much use. . . . They thought they were eating and drinking only the sort of things you might find in a stable. One said he was trying to eat hay. . . .

"You see," said Aslan. "They will not let us help them. They have chosen cunning instead of belief. Their prison is only in their own minds, yet they are in that prison; and so afraid of being taken in that they cannot be taken out."

LB: 168–169

"It's rather late to be thinking of precautions now that we're inside and the door shut behind us."

SC: 107

"Be careful, Pole. It's just the sort of place that might lead to a dragon's cave. And in a giant country, there might be giant earth-worms or giant beetles."

SC: 99

"Steady pace, now. . . . Don't look frightened, whatever you do. We've done the silliest thing in the world by coming at all: but now that we *are* here, we'd best put a bold face on it."

SC: 104

SC: 68

The Effect of Beauty

In the darkness something was happening at last. A voice had begun to sing. . . . Its lower notes were deep enough to be the voice of the earth herself. There were no words. There was hardly even a tune. But it was, beyond comparison, the most beautiful noise [Digory] had ever heard. It was so beautiful he could hardly bear it. . . .

"Glory be!" said the Cabby. "I'd ha' been a better man all my life if I'd known there were things like this."

MN: 106–7

Faith

"It *is* all a dream," said the Witch, always thrumming. . . . "There is no Narnia, no Overworld, no sky, no sun, no Aslan."

—*Queen of Underland*

SC: 176 & 180

SC: 177

"One word, Ma'am," [Puddleglum] said. . . . "Suppose we *have* only dreamed, or made up, all those things. . . . Then all I can say is that, in that case, the made-up things seem a good deal more important than the real ones. . . . That's why I'm going to stand by the play-world. I'm on Aslan's side even if there isn't any Aslan to lead it. I'm going to live as like a Narnian as I can even if there isn't any Narnia."

SC: 181–182

SC: 166

There might be fruit in some other world that would really cure his mother. . . . And he had the magic rings. There must be worlds you could get to through every pool in the wood. He could hunt through them all. And then—*Mother well again*. Everything right again.

MN: 92–93

MN: 197

"I have come home at last! This is my real country! I belong here. This is the land I have been looking for all my life, though I never knew it till now."

—*Jewel the Unicorn*

LB: 196

LB: 77

VDT: 32

"My own plans are made. While I can, I sail east in the *Dawn Treader*. When she fails me, I paddle east in my coracle. When she sinks, I shall swim east with my four paws. And when I can swim no longer, if I have not reached Aslan's country . . . I shall sink with my nose to the sunrise and Peepiceek will be head of the talking mice in Narnia."

—*Reepicheep*

VDT: 213

LB: 177

The End & the Beginning

And for us this is the end of all the stories, and we can most truly say that they all lived happily ever after. But for them it was only the beginning of the real story. All their life in this world and all their adventures in Narnia had only been the cover and the title page: now at last they were beginning Chapter One of the Great Story which no one on earth has read: which goes on forever: in which every chapter is better than the one before.

"The term is over: the holidays have begun. The dream is ended: this is the morning."

—*Aslan*

LB: 210

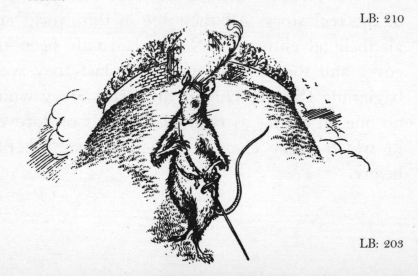

LB: 203